Feel Great and Look Your Best

Anti-Inflammatory Recipes

Margaret Boyd-Squires
BHSc (Naturopathy)

This book is dedicated to my husband Frankie and my kids, Rocky and Sienna. Thank you for waiting for your meals all those countless times while I took photos or perfected a recipe. All your enthusiasm and ideas for the book helped to keep me going. Thank you Frankie for walking with me through this journey and for all your help in making this idea a reality. You are all my light, love and laughter.

X Margaret

PS - Thanks to my dog Toffee, also known as Mr Fluff, who kept me company on the late nights I stayed up working on the book. And finaly, thanks also to my patients, many of whom have been seeing me for years, who helped inspire me to write this book.

 A catalogue record for this book is available from the National Library of Australia

Copyright © 2018 Margaret Boyd-Squires

All rights reserved worldwide.

No part of the book may be copied or changed in any format, sold, or used in a way other than what is outlined in this book, under any circumstances, without the prior written permission of the publisher.

Publisher:
ASPG (Australian Self Publishing Group)
P.O. Box 159, Calwell, ACT Australia 2905
Email: publishaspg@gmail.com
http://www.inspiringpublishers.com
National Library of Australia Cataloguing-in-Publication entry

Author: Boyd-Squires, Margaret

Title: **Feel Great and Look Your Best:** Anti-Inflammatory Recipes/*Margaret Boyd-Squires.*

ISBN: 978-0-6483529-5-2 (pbk)

Disclaimer:

This book intends to educate and teach people about how they can use certain foods to overcome common disorders. The reader takes all responsibility for her/ his use of the material written in the book.

The result expressed in the book can vary, depending on how people use it.

The views and advice expressed in this book are not intended to be a substitute for conventional medical services. If you have any concerns regarding your (or your loved one's) condition, see your physician of choice.

MARGARET BOYD-SQUIRES is a passionate Naturopath who believes wholeheartedly in food as medicine. This book came about because of the increasingly high levels of inflammation she saw in her patients. She saw a need for a simple book to teach them about the foods to include in their diet to reduce inflammation, and how to use them in everyday recipes. Margaret is degree qualified and has been in practice for 24 years. She is 48 years old and lives with her husband and two children in Melbourne, Australia.

She lives in the real world too, and is busy like the rest of us, so her recipes are simple and her advice is down to earth. She hopes to inspire others so that they too can feel great and look their best.

CONTENTS

INTRODUCTION 9

BREAKFAST 15

LUNCH 23

DIPS 33

SNACKS 37

SIDE DISHES 41

SALADS 55

SOUP 67

DINNER 73

HOME REMEDIES 93

THINGS YOU SHOULD KNOW 97

INDEX 101

Anti-Inflammatory Recipes

INTRODUCTION

INTRODUCTION

I have been in practice for 24 years and in working with patients I have increasingly come to see the huge role that inflammation is playing in their symptoms. Inflammation is believed to be a driver of disease and therefore slowing down the inflammatory process is imperative for a long life. Inflammation increases naturally as we age, so if we can reduce inflammation we will slow the aging process. I believe an anti-inflammatory diet is totally achievable whilst still living in the real world and indulging once in a while. In this book I will give you recipes that are easy, tasty, focused on reducing inflammation and I am including explanations and tips on how to achieve a longer, less inflammatory life.

Research is increasingly finding that inflammation is a driver of many diseases. From serious diseases such as heart disease, type 2 diabetes, Alzheimer's and cancer to the more common diseases that are extremely debilitating, such as inflammatory bowel disease, polycystic ovarian syndrome, auto-immune disease and many more. Common presentations of inflammation that I see in clinic are tiredness and adrenal exhaustion, bloating, hormonal imbalance, acne and headaches. Generally I see many people of all ages who are carrying extra weight (usually around the middle), who feel they are prematurely ageing, and feel sluggish, achey and tired.

So what are anti-inflammatory foods? Generally speaking, an anti-inflammatory diet consists of vegetables, fruit, legumes, healthy fats, herbs and spices, nuts and seeds, fish, and unrefined complex grains. On the other hand, an inflammatory diet consists of refined sugar and flour, colours and preservatives, excesses of red meat, alcohol and bread, fried foods, and saturated fats. This is very general of course but I think you get the idea – natural, unprocessed foods that are high in fibre and nutrients are anti-inflammatory while processed and refined foods that are no longer fresh are inflammatory.

I believe in following the 80:20 rule – keep the diet really healthy 80% of the time and you will get away with indulging 20%. It is the dietary habits you adhere to the majority of the time that really affect the direction your health goes. So if you can follow an anti-inflammatory way of eating 80% of the time you will get away with indulging 20% and still keep inflammation down.

Indulge once in a while, it is really important for your sanity. Do remember though, that a lot of the foods we indulge in are quite addictive so know that when you do this you will need to rein yourself in, or next thing you know, these foods will become the majority. Often people need to mentally put the inflammatory foods that they like to eat into the 'treat' category. This can help as you are not depriving yourself but rather realising that these foods shouldn't be eaten too often.

One of the things I see in my practice which contributes to inflammation is that many people eat too often and too much. I believe we need to give our digestion a break from food every so often so that our body can carry out some general housekeeping. Reducing portion size is another good idea and the easiest way to start off weight loss. Reducing portion size and having small periods where you take a break from eating will also reduce inflammation. After you focus on this, you can then add in more anti-inflammatory foods and you will really start to feel better.

INTRODUCTION

Inflammation is like a ball rolling down a hill, once it starts it is quite hard to stop, so be patient with an anti-inflammatory diet. You will feel better for eating this way rather quickly but it may take a little longer for inflammatory health issues to improve.

By the way, when it comes to weight loss I believe it is 80% diet and 20% exercise. I see far too many people who are exercising a lot who are still carrying a lot of unhealthy weight and inflammation. Exercise is very important for overall health and weight loss, but if weight gain is your issue I would advise focusing foremost on your diet and follow this up with consistent exercise.

If you can find a way to do it, grow your own vegetables and herbs. It will improve your health on two levels – the gardening will keep you fit and the fresh vegetables grown without chemicals and taken straight to your table will help keep you healthy. Not to mention you will eat a more anti-inflammatory diet because you will have many vegetables that need to be eaten. You don't need the perfect spot for a vegie garden either. My vegie garden gives me enormous joy and lots of fresh produce even though it's not in the best spot for growing. If you don't have anywhere to grow outside you can always grow vegies or herbs on your balcony, on your windowsill, or in a vertical garden. Microgreens, which are an incredible source of nutrition, are especially easy to grow and can be grown indoors all year round and outdoors in summer. Watching plants grow gives you enormous satisfaction as well as saves you money and ensures there are no chemicals or pesticides in your food.

You will notice lots of fresh herbs in all these recipes. These, of course, come from my garden, and fresh herbs are what make the difference in flavor when you are following an anti-inflammatory diet. Herbs are full of nutrients such as iron, folate and antioxidants. They have healing properties as well. For example the mints will aid digestion, coriander is a powerful heavy metal chelator and basil is anti-inflammatory. It's worth going to the trouble to find fresh turmeric root (it's not too hard these days, you'll find it at the greengrocer). Turmeric is incredibly anti-inflammatory and it adds beautiful warmth to dishes. It is best stored in the fridge and will last 2-3 weeks loosely wrapped in dry paper towel. Turmeric powder is still useful for its anti-inflammatory properties, but the fresh root is far superior as fresh herbs are more potent. Equally, fresh ginger root is a must have. It also adds warmth to a dish and it aids digestion whilst also having anti-inflammatory properties.

Organisation is key to a consistently healthy anti-inflammatory diet. Go shopping regularly or else do one big shop, but make sure your fridge and cupboards are always full. Plan your meals ahead or just have some consistent anti-inflammatory meals that you cycle through during the week. Have salad leaves washed, dried and in bags or containers ready to go in the fridge. They last for about 5 days and make it easy for you to quickly make a salad. Celery is one of the most alkaline of vegetables, and your body uses more energy to break it down than it actually gets from it, so it's perfect for weight loss. I wash an entire head of celery each week, cut it into pieces and put in a covered bowl of water in the fridge. It keeps for nearly a week and will be very crunchy, ready for use in salads, for a snack with hummus or to use in cooking.

INTRODUCTION

   Another routine to get into is to do a big 'freezer' cook each weekend. Of course, it is better not to freeze meals at all but if you are time poor and it's a choice between a healthy freezer meal and take-away, I know which I would choose. If you do this consistently you will have a full freezer very soon and this will save you on nights you get home late and need food on the table quickly. These time savers are good routines to get into and after a while they just become the prep work for the week.
   Add apple cider vinegar to your diet. You will find it in many of the salad dressings and recipes in this book. It is anti-inflammatory, alkalising, and great for the metabolism. Drink a teaspoon of apple cider vinegar twice daily in a glass of water and along with an anti-inflammatory diet and exercise you will start to see your metabolism changing.
   Another thing to add to your diet is psyllium. It can be taken in a large glass of water or else see my breakfast recipes where psyllium is included. Psyllium has supreme health properties. As well as being a prebiotic food for the growth of probiotics, it is a soluble fibre that bulks up the bowel movement and improves the peristaltic motion of the bowel. Due to the nature of the strands of fibre in psyllium, it is like a 'toothbrush' for the bowel and can help to remove toxins from the bowel wall and lower cholesterol as well. Remember, you are what you eat but also what you excrete, and a bowel that functions well will keep inflammation down, reduce toxicity in the body and help you to have a good metabolism.
   I tend to make large quantities when I cook during the week so I can use the leftovers over the next day or so. This way, I avoid unhealthy lunches that have to be bought because I have nothing prepared. Making big quantities is your best friend, it not only saves you money and time but it will also help to keep inflammation levels down consistently.
   Be careful with eating out as this can be your undoing when trying to eat an anti-inflammatory diet. It's important to spend time with family and friends but I suggest you look at how many times a week eating out at a restaurant occurs, and see if it takes you out of you 80:20 balance. Of course, you can seek out a healthier restaurant, but there is a lot to be said for knowing exactly what went into the meal and what quality of oils were used, information which is hard to glean from a menu. The majority of restaurant offerings are not anti-inflammatory foods, so enjoy them but not too often.
   Regarding oils in this recipe book, you will notice that I try to avoid cooking oils as much as I can, but some recipes do require a small amount of oil. In these recipes, I choose to use coconut oil as it has a high smoking point and therefore won't oxidise at high temperatures as other oils do. This oxidisation creates free radicals that increase inflammation and can damage the body. Even olive oil with all its good properties is not the best oil to heat. Coconut oil has many good properties but it is high in saturated fat so you still need to keep it to a minimum. There are two types of coconut oil. Unrefined coconut oil will impart a coconut flavor to a dish so I use it in dishes that benefit from the coconut flavor. Refined coconut oil has no flavor so it is better if you do not like or want

INTRODUCTION

a coconut flavor. It is a good idea to keep both in the cupboard (unless you don't like coconut at all, then just keep refined). For uncooked oils to use in salads, etc., I use either extra-virgin olive oil or flaxseed oil, both of which have excellent health properties.

Except for a couple of recipes that include pork, I have largely left red meat out of this cookbook. It's not because red meat is all bad, but because I find a lot of people have way too much of it, and in large quantities it is inflammatory. In this recipe book I want to introduce you to the things you can include in your diet to reduce inflammation but by all means eat red meat if you wish, just keep the quantities down.

Please don't be upset with me but I have not included a dessert section. The reason for this is that desserts are generally inflammatory since they are sweet and have some form of sugar in them. Even if they have healthy sugars they are still inflammatory. For your desserts if you choose to have them, you will need to use one of your other cookbooks (not one focusing on anti-inflammatory recipes) and then put this dessert into your 20% and indulge.

As boring as it sounds, moderation is the key. It's less about what you take out of your diet but more about what you focus on putting in. Reduce the inflammatory foods and increase the anti-inflammatory foods and you will reduce inflammation, lose weight, slow the aging process, prevent disease and feel better.

Enjoy the recipes in this book, your body will thank you.

Margaret

*except for the photo of me, all photos in this book were taken by me with my iPhone in my kitchen using my existing crockery with no lighting or photographic tricks.

BREAKFAST

Gluten-Free Breakfast Cereal

Gluten-Free Breakfast Cereal

This cereal is particularly high in fibre. It has the added benefit of being gluten-free so it is suitable for those who have to avoid gluten. For the rest of us, it is good to include some gluten-free foods in our diet, as gluten can be quite inflammatory for the gut. Buckwheat is a member of the rhubarb family and despite its name it doesn't contain any wheat or gluten. It is included in the cereal as it is high in protein, fibre and nutrients. Amaranth and quinoa are also included as they are both high in protein, fibre, nutrients and good oils. Psyllium husks are a soluble fibre that works by absorbing water to become a mucilage and therefore improves the peristaltic motion of the bowel. It is like a 'toothbrush' for the bowel with its ability to clean the bowel wall. It can also help to reduce cholesterol and will help your bowel movements to be more regular and well formed. I make this with a mixture of dried goji berries and blueberries, both of which are very good for you and contain less sugar than other dried fruits. The high fibre content in this muesli helps to balance your gut microbiome by providing prebiotic food for the growth of good bacteria. A well functioning bowel will help to reduce inflammation and toxicity in the body, and overall improve your metabolism.

- 250 g rice bran cereal (sometimes called rice bran straws)
- 100 g puffed buckwheat
- 100 g puffed amaranth
- 100 g puffed quinoa
- 100 g psyllium husks
- 150 g LSA meal
- 100 g desiccated (or flaked) coconut
- 200 g dried fruit of your choice e.g. goji berries, blueberries, apricots
- 100 g pumpkin seeds

Combine and store in large glass airtight containers (you will require approximately two large containers).

Serve with the milk of your choice. Alternatively use in my *Yoghurt and Muesli* recipe on page 19.

Keeps for at least 6 weeks.

Margaret's Blueberry Nut Muesli

This muesli is high in protein, and high in soluble fibre and nutrients. I choose dried blueberries for this recipe because they are a lower glycemic fruit (meaning it is digested more slowly and therefore causes a slower rise in blood sugar and insulin levels which is a good thing). Blueberries are also extremely high in antioxidants. Psyllium is once again added to the muesli because of its supreme health properties. As well as being a prebiotic food for the growth of probiotics, it is also a soluble fibre that bulks up the bowel movement. Psyllium can help to remove toxins form the bowel wall and lower cholesterol.

- 750 g wholegrain or organic rolled oats
- 350 mls apple juice or another fruit juice of your choice
- 5 tablespoons organic unrefined coconut oil
- 225 g raw almonds, whole
- 110 g sunflower seeds
- 120 g pumpkin seeds
- 120 g sesame seeds (white)
- 280 g dried blueberries
- 120 g hazelnuts, halved with kitchen scissors
- 160 g quinoa flakes
- 130 g psyllium husks

Preheat oven to 160°C fan forced. Mix all the ingredients together in a very large bowl except for the dried blueberries and the psyllium husks.

Mix well and distribute out into two large fairly deep oven trays, one oven tray will do but it toasts more evenly if you spread it over two trays. Stir half way and cook for approximately 45 minutes or until golden brown. Allow to cool completely before adding the blueberries and psyllium husks. Stir well.

Store in large glass airtight containers (fills approximately two large glass containers depending on size).

Makes a large quantity, which gets eaten in my house, just halve the batch if you think this will be too much.

Serve with the milk or yoghurt of your choice, or alternatively have it as I do, with my *Yoghurt and Muesli* recipe on page 19.

Keeps for at least 6 weeks.

> **Tip:** To make a gluten-free version, substitute the oats for another 750 g of quinoa flakes (910 g quinoa flakes in total) and cook them just as the recipe suggests you do with the oats. Generally though, for those not actually intolerant or allergic to gluten, the amount of gluten in this muesli is low and oats do have lots of good health properties.

Anti-Inflammatory Recipes

Quinoa and Vegetable Scramble

I often have leftover cooked quinoa in the fridge and with its high protein and soluble fibre content, it is great to add to eggs and vegetables for breakfast (or lunch). You can vary the vegetables in this according to what you have on hand. By adding vegetables and quinoa to your scrambled eggs it's easier to skip having toast with it, and it will keep you fuller for longer.

- 2 free-range eggs
- Dash of the milk of your choice
- 1 small handful fresh or dried mixed herbs such as chives, Vietnamese mint, parsley, basil
- Sea salt and pepper to taste
- 2 mushrooms, sliced
- 10 cm stalk of celery, sliced thinly
- ¼ green capsicum, sliced thinly into small pieces
- 2 tablespoons cooked quinoa (see page 98 for cooking instructions)

Whisk the eggs, milk, herbs and salt and pepper in a small bowl.

Add the vegetables to a very hot pan and cook, stirring for a few minutes. I don't add any oil as I find it's not necessary, I just stir a lot. Once the vegetables are softened a little add the egg mixture and stir quickly for a couple of minutes or until the eggs are cooked.

Add the cooked quinoa to the egg and vegetables and stir for 2 minutes to warm the quinoa.

Place the vegetables, egg and quinoa on a plate and serve with a small amount of sliced avocado and rocket if you wish.

SERVES 1

Yoghurt and Muesli

The following is a breakfast I often put together because it is high in protein, good fats and fibre. Flaxseed oil contains omega 3 fatty acids that have numerous health benefits for the brain, heart, hair and skin. Flaxseed oil can also help with the movement of the bowel and most importantly, it can help to reduce inflammation. LSA contains a blend of linseeds, sunflower seeds and almonds. You can grind it yourself if you are able (you will get more good fats this way) but the next best thing is to buy it already ground. LSA is high in good fats, protein and nutrients. Lecithin has good health properties as it contains many nutrients and pumpkin seeds are a good source of zinc. This breakfast will keep you full for hours due to the high levels of protein, fibre and fat and it ticks all the boxes for keeping you slim.

2 heaped tablespoons fat-free yoghurt
1 tablespoon flaxseed oil
1 teaspoon LSA meal (store in a jar in the fridge)
1 teaspoon lecithin granules (store in a jar in the fridge)
1 heaped tablespoon *Margaret's Blueberry Nut Muesli* (see page 17) OR
1 heaped tablespoon *Gluten-Free Breakfast Cereal* (see page 16)
1 teaspoon pumpkin seeds (store in a jar in the fridge)
Small amount berries (either blueberries, raspberries, strawberries or blackberries – stick with fresh rather than frozen)

Combine and enjoy.

Tip: I like to squish the berries so that it turns a red/ purple colour depending on the berry; it seems to add to the taste too!

SERVES 1

Sienna's Maple Berry Muesli for Kids

Sienna's Maple Berry Muesli for Kids

Healthy foods sometimes have to be altered a little to suit children's palates. This is an adaption of my *Blueberry Nut Muesli* that is more suited for kids. It has a little more natural sugar and natural fat, but it ticks all the boxes for soluble fibre, protein, and nutrients. Of course, there are no colors, preservatives or refined sugar, which are found in most supermarket muesli. Children will use the extra natural sugars and fat due to their activity levels and this muesli will get them off to school ready for a big day. Children love it served with Greek Yoghurt or else with the milk of their choice. I find they really benefit from the psyllium and fibre in this muesli as many parents bring their children to see me regarding their constipated or sluggish bowel. Amaranth is native to Peru and is gluten-free, high in protein, fibre, nutrients and good oils. I make this at the same time as my *Blueberry Nut Muesli* for adults. This muesli smells so good while it is cooking.

- 500 g wholegrain or organic rolled oats
- 30 g organic puffed amaranth
- 50 g organic quinoa puffed
- 30 g organic puffed buckwheat
- 100 g pumpkin seeds
- 60 g sesame seeds (white)
- 60 g desiccated (or flaked) coconut
- 3 tablespoons organic unrefined coconut oil
- 3 tablespoons quality maple syrup
- 300 g dried blueberries
- 80 g psyllium husks

Preheat the oven to 160°C fan forced. Place the oats, amaranth, quinoa, buckwheat, pumpkin and sesame seeds, and coconut in a large oven tray.

Put the coconut oil and maple syrup in a small pan and stir over medium heat until dissolved.

Pour the coconut oil and maple syrup mixture over the dry ingredients in the pan and stir well to combine.

Cook for approximately 40 minutes at 160 °C stirring half way so that it cooks evenly. Once golden brown remove from the oven and allow to cool. Once cooled completely add the psyllium and the dried blueberries.

Store in a large glass airtight container (fills approximately one large container depending on size).

Keeps for at least 6 weeks.

Quick Quinoa Porridge

This breakfast is perfect in winter when you need something to warm you up. It is super quick to make, taking just 5 minutes from start to finish. You can also vary this recipe a lot. I tend to use almond milk and fresh blueberries but you can use the milk and fresh fruit of your choice. It is a breakfast that is slightly higher in carbs but we do tend to need slightly more carbs in winter. It's not short on protein though, as the almond milk contains protein and so does the quinoa and LSA. This breakfast is also high in fibre and nutrients and will sit well in your stomach. As a variation of traditional porridge, this version has the benefit of being gluten-free and higher in protein.

- 1 cup almond milk (or coconut milk, rice milk or any milk of your choice)
- ⅓ cup quinoa flakes
- Pinch of sea salt
- ¼ cup fresh berries or fruit of your choice
- 1 teaspoon LSA meal (linseed, sunflower and almond meal)

Have everything ready to go before you start as the quinoa cooks quickly. Bring the milk to a boil over medium heat. When the milk comes to a boil quickly add the quinoa flakes, a pinch of salt and the LSA. Give it a quick stir and turn off the heat. Stir again until combined and leave to sit for 2 or 3 minutes to allow the quinoa to cook.

Stir again, it will now be nice and thick and creamy, and serve with the fresh fruit on top.

SERVES 1

Chicken Rice Paper Rolls

I often bring these along to picnics as they can be prepared beforehand, but they work equally well as an entrée, a light dinner or a standard lunch. I either use a free-range roast chicken which I have bought or else I roast a chicken myself. I find you don't need the noodles which are often put in rice paper rolls. These rice paper rolls are low in carb content, high in protein and the addition of cabbage, which is incredibly good for you, makes them anti-inflammatory. As well as having anti-inflammatory properties, cabbage is high in calcium and is thought to be cancer preventative. They are gluten-free, quick to make, and they taste delicious!

Rice paper rounds, 16 cm size, most packs contain many rice papers, you will need approximately 40
½ cabbage, shredded
1 quality free-range or organic cooked roast chicken, shredded
Tarragon, fresh if possible, 4 sprigs or 1½ tablespoons dried
Mint, fresh if possible, 4 sprigs or 1½ tablespoons dried

Dipping sauce:
1 tablespoon fish sauce
2 tablespoons lime juice
2 red bird's eye chillis deseeded and finely sliced
2 tablespoons apple cider vinegar
1 teaspoon honey
1 tablespoon sesame seeds

Wet a tea towel and place it over a cutting board. Boil the kettle and allow to cool a little before filling a bowl with the hot water. Soak one rice paper round in the hot water until it softens, remove from the water and place a small amount of the shredded chicken, lots of cabbage and a pinch of tarragon and mint at the top of the round. Fold the two sides over and roll toward you into a cigar shape. Make sure to replace each rice paper round with a new one in the bowl of warm water so that you have a steady stream of softened rice paper and a quick production line.

Combine all the ingredients for the dipping sauce in a small bowl.

The dipping sauce is delicious, but if you are short on time simply serve the rice paper rolls with a chilli or sweet chilli sauce.

SERVES 4

Chick Pea Tuna Salad

This simple salad is high in protein and full of fibre and nutrients. It is quick and easy to make. Apple cider vinegar is in the dressing and it is very good for your gut and your metabolism – a good thing to include in your diet for overall gut health and weight loss. It is also tangy and delicious especially when put with the seeded mustard in the dressing. Kids love this salad because of its simple flavours and it works well in their lunchboxes too. This salad also is great for dinner when you just want something light.

- 2 x 400 g cans organic chick peas, rinsed and drained
- 1 cucumber, sliced and quartered
- ¼ of a small red onion, thinly sliced and diced
- 1 stalk of celery including any young green tops, sliced and halved
- 3 medium mushrooms, sliced and quartered
- A handful of fresh chopped herbs such as parsley, chives, mint, tarragon, Vietnamese mint, any or all of these if you have them
- 1 medium size can of tuna (185 g)

Dressing:
- 1 ½ tablespoons seeded mustard
- 2 tablespoons organic apple cider vinegar
- 3 teaspoons flaxseed oil
- Sea salt and pepper to taste

Combine all ingredients and enjoy.

SERVES 4

Quinoa Sushi Rolls

Quinoa Sushi Rolls

These sushi rolls are gluten-free, high in protein, fibre, good fats and nutrients. As well as this they taste great, are good in kids' lunches and picnics, and they really impress when you make them for others. Rolling them is easier than you think, just pick up a bamboo mat from the supermarket to make the job easy. Cook the quinoa way before you plan to assemble them as it has to completely cool. The beetroot and sesame really make this recipe but feel free to change the fillings according to what you have, make a vegetarian version, the sky is the limit.

- 1 bamboo mat
- 1 cup uncooked quinoa
- 1½ cups water
- ½ cup apple cider vinegar
- 2 teaspoons honey
- 1 teaspoon Celtic sea salt
- 185 g can tuna
- ½ lemon
- Celtic sea salt and cracked pepper
- 6 sheets nori seaweed
- 1 ripe avocado, pitted peeled and sliced
- 1 Lebanese cucumber, cut into sticks
- 1 medium beetroot, peeled and julienned
- Black (or white) sesame seeds

To serve (optional)
   Tamari, Wasabi, Sriracha Chilli Sauce or Sambal Asli Chilli Sauce

Rinse the quinoa and add to a medium saucepan with the water. Bring to a boil then lower the heat and simmer, covered for approximately 15 minutes. Meanwhile put the apple cider vinegar, honey and salt in a small saucepan over medium heat, bring to a simmer and keep warm until the quinoa is ready. When 15 minutes have passed and the water has been absorbed by the quinoa, add the vinegar mixture and stir well whilst still on the heat. Leave on the heat, cover again and after 5-10 minutes the quinoa will have absorbed the liquid. Remove from the heat, stir, and allow to cool completely.

Drain the tuna and add the lemon, salt and pepper to taste, mix well.

To assemble the sushi rolls, lay the bamboo mat on a flat surface and place plastic wrap over the top. Lay one sheet of nori (shiny side down) on top of the plastic and spread 1/6 of the quinoa on top of the nori, leaving a border at all four edges. Place the fillings in the bottom third of the nori, first the avocado, then cucumber, beetroot, tuna and a sprinkle of sesame seeds making sure to use about 1/6 of the fillings (be careful not to overfill). Pick up the mat closest to you and fold it over, pressing as you go, pull it toward you, and then keep rolling and pressing. If the final edge doesn't stick wet it with water. Cut the rolls with a very sharp knife in the middle to make hand rolls, or else cut into smaller pieces. Serve plain or with sauces of your choice.

MAKES 12 HAND ROLLS

Flavoursome Poached Chicken

This is a quick lunch and all you need is to have a chicken breast on hand, best fresh of course but even if you keep a single chicken breast in the freezer you can always whip up a quick, low fat, high protein and very tasty lunch. Once poached the chicken is full of flavour and very tender. This can be cooking while you make the dinner with no real effort and then you just have to slice it up and put it with a leftover salad and you have lunch for the next day done.

1 boneless, skinless, quality chicken breast preferably free range and/ or organic
1 good sized clove of garlic, sliced roughly
½ teaspoon fennel seeds
½ teaspoon dried tarragon
½ teaspoon Italian herbs
½ teaspoon cumin, ground

Place the chicken breast in a pot of water so that the chicken is covered completely. Add the garlic, fennel seeds and tarragon, Italian herbs and cumin and bring to the boil. Reduce heat to low and simmer, covered, for approximately 15 minutes or until cooked through (always good to check the middle is cooked). Turn off the heat and leave to sit in the liquid with the lid on for five minutes. Slice thinly and you are done. Serve with a salad, Asian greens or with steamed vegetables.

> You can really play around with the flavours in this recipe, but this is a very tasty combination.

SERVES 1

Tamari Silken Tofu

This is a very quick lunch to prepare and it's easy to always have tofu on hand in the fridge. Tofu is fairly tasteless but it takes on the flavours you add to it. Silken tofu melts in your mouth and is the best tofu to use in this dish. As well as this lunch being quick to make, it is high in protein and low in fat.

- 300 g silken tofu (GMO free)
- Tamari to drizzle
- Lemon juice from a quarter of a lemon
- Sea salt and pepper to taste
- Optional: chopped herbs such as coriander, Vietnamese mint, basil, parsley

Steam the tofu in a steamer for 5 minutes (can also be steamed in the microwave by placing the tofu in a bowl of water for 5 minutes, obviously for health reasons it is best done in a steamer).

Remove the tofu quickly and slice thinly. Generously drizzle the tamari, a small amount of lemon juice, salt and pepper and scatter chopped herbs if you have them on top.

Tip: Serve with steamed greens such as chinese broccoli, bok choy or broccolini, or simply serve with a salad (hopefully left over from last night).

SERVES 1

Cauliflower and Cumin Scramble

Cauliflower and Cumin Scramble

Cauliflower is a highly anti-inflammatory vegetable as it has very high levels of antioxidants and nutrients and as part of the *Brassica* family it is thought to prevent cancer. This recipe has a very tasty flavour combination, the cauliflower is slightly crunchy and the cumin adds a mild warmth to the dish. This lunch sits very well in your stomach, leaving it feel warm and content and it is excellent for breakfast too.

- 2 free-range eggs
- Dash of low-fat milk (or almond, rice or coconut milk)
- ½ teaspoon cumin, ground
- ½ teaspoon dried parsley or a few sprigs fresh parsley
- Sea salt and pepper to taste
- 100 g cauliflower, chopped into small pieces
- Avocado slices: optional
- Microgreens or rocket to garnish

Whisk the eggs, milk, cumin, parsley and salt and pepper in a small bowl.

Add the cauliflower to a very hot pan and reduce the heat immediately to medium. No need for oil, just stir frequently for 5 minutes allowing the cauliflower to brown a little.

Turn up the heat to high and add the egg mixture to the cauliflower and stir quickly for a few minutes or until the eggs are cooked.

Place the cauliflower eggs onto a plate and add a few slices of avocado if you wish and garnish with microgreens or your favourite fresh herb.

SERVES 1

DIPS

Avocado Dip with Garlic and Chilli, Margaret's Hummus and Eggplant Dip

Margaret's Hummus

Chickpeas are high in protein, fibre and nutrients. This hummus is quick to make, much nicer than store bought hummus, and great as a snack or as part of a mezze. Eaten with celery sticks or rice crackers it makes a great high protein snack. I use organic canned chick peas when I make this, but if you have the time, use dried chick peas. Soak them overnight, drain and add to a large pot and cover with several inches of water. Simmer for approximately 1½ hours, until tender.

- 800 g organic chick peas (2 x 400 g cans, rinsed and drained)
- 3 cloves garlic
- 2 level teaspoons Celtic sea salt
- 1 small hot red chilli or 1 large medium red chilli (seeds removed)
- 2 level teaspoons cumin, ground
- 1 ½ - 2 lemons, juiced
- 1 tablespoon organic hulled tahini (not the oil)
- ½ cup extra virgin olive oil
- Smoked paprika to sprinkle on top

Blend all the ingredients except the lemon juice in a food processor. Add the lemon slowly as you may not need all the lemon juice. Add extra chilli or garlic if you wish.

Serve in a shallow dish and sprinkle with smoked paprika.

Lasts 4 days in an airtight container in the fridge.

SERVES 4

Tip: Add a small amount of raw beetroot and blend with the hummus to turn it into beetroot hummus.

Eggplant Dip

Eggplants contain an impressive array of nutrients including anti-inflammatory antioxidants. They also contain very few calories and lots of fibre making them excellent for weight loss and overall health. This has a smoky flavor and is worth the 45 minutes or so that it takes to make.

- 3 medium to large eggplants
- 3 tablespoons organic hulled tahini (not the oil)
- 1 tablespoon warm water
- 1 teaspoon Celtic sea salt
- Juice of 1 to 1 ½ lemons
- 3 cloves garlic finely grated
- ½ teaspoon cumin, ground
- Sweet paprika to sprinkle on top
- Small handful of flat leaf parsley to garnish

Prick the eggplants all around with a fork and cook them on a very hot griddle until blackened on the outside and soft inside (no oil required just place them directly on the griddle). You will need to turn them frequently. This takes approximately half an hour. Cooking them on the griddle gives the dip a smoky flavor. Alternatively, once pricked, you can cook them in the oven at 210°C for about an hour.

Leave the eggplants to cool. Put a sieve over a bowl and once the eggplants are cool enough to handle, break the eggplants open and spoon out the pulp into the sieve. Use a fork to push out the liquid and mash the eggplant. Leave to drain over the bowl for approximately 15 minutes.

In a large bowl, mix the tahini with the tablespoon of warm water and mix using a fork. Mix in the sea salt and then stir in some of the lemon juice until all is well combined. Add the eggplant to this, and then the garlic and cumin and mix well. Add lemon juice slowly to taste and additional sea salt if needed. Serve in a shallow serving bowl with a few shakes of sweet paprika on top and garnish with the parsley.

Lasts 4 days in an airtight container in the fridge.

SERVES 6

Avocado Dip with Garlic and Chilli

The health benefits of avocado are well known and don't need much introduction, but it is worth mentioning that their high levels of good fats are anti-inflammatory. This dip is quick and easy to make and totally worth it as it is so delicious. Great to use as a standalone dip or else as a guacamole to serve with corn chips or Mexican dishes. I tend to go overboard with the garlic, and if you can tolerate garlic and enjoy it, this tastes delicious with three large cloves.

- 2 avocados
- ½ lemon, juiced
- 2 garlic cloves (or 3 if you love garlic)
- 4 drops Tabasco sauce
- Dash of sweet chilli sauce
- Herbamare seasoning to taste (a seasoning salt made from herbs and vegetables)
- Pepper to taste

Blend all ingredients with a stick blender until smooth.

Serve in a shallow dish and garnish with microgreens or fresh coriander.

Lasts 4 days in an airtight container in the fridge.

SERVES 4

Tip: This goes well in a Buddha bowl, a current trend, which I have been calling my 'bits and pieces' lunch for years. A Buddha bowl simply consists of healthy, anti-inflammatory bits and pieces including dips (hopefully home made), a small amount of a complex grain such as quinoa, raw vegies and salads, legumes and perhaps some tofu or chicken. It should include lots of colours and if you take the time to arrange it well, it not only looks great but is a balanced anti-inflammatory meal.

SNACKS

The Real Deal Muesli Bars

The Real Deal Muesli Bars

Mass-produced muesli bars are generally low in protein and incredibly high in sugar, preservatives and gluten. These are very tasty, easy to make, and worth the effort as the amount of gluten is low, and with buckwheat on board, the good fats, nutrients and protein are higher. Egg, berries and seeds further add to the protein and nutrients. These are fun to make and you will question why you buy the mass produced type. Good for adults and kids. Kids can have a whole bar but adults don't need as much energy, so cut the bar in half and have half as a snack, that's if you want to stay trim/ lose weight (the half bar will keep you full for quite a while).

- 80 g multigrain or organic oats
- 50 g puffed buckwheat
- 40 g whole raw almonds, chopped small with a knife
- 20 g fine desiccated coconut
- 20 g dried goji berries
- 20 g dried blueberries
- 20 g white sesame seeds
- 20 g pumpkin seeds
- 2 eggs
- 3 tablespoons good quality honey
- 3 tablespoons unrefined coconut oil
- ¼ teaspoon Celtic sea salt

Preheat the oven to 130°C fan forced. Lightly grease a 23 cm x 32 cm tin and line the base with baking paper. Put the oats, buckwheat, chopped almonds, coconut, goji and blueberries, sesame and pumpkin seeds in a large bowl.

Whisk the eggs in a bowl and add the sea salt.

Put the honey and coconut oil in a small pan and stir over medium heat until dissolved.

Pour the whisked eggs into the oats, buckwheat, almonds, coconut, dried fruit and seeds mixture and combine well. Pour the dissolved honey and coconut in and combine.

Spoon the mixture into the lined tin and press down with a potato masher until firmly in place.

Bake for about 35 minutes or until golden brown. Remove from the oven and leave for a couple of minutes. Using a knife, cut while hot into bars approximately 3 cm x 11 cm. Press down again once cut with your hands and place in the fridge for 40 minutes. Remove the muesli bars with a flat spatula and store in a container.

MAKES 18 MUESLI BARS

Lime, Chilli and Paprika Pepitas

Otherwise known as pumpkin seeds, pepitas are high in zinc, magnesium, fibre, protein and good fats. All of this makes them a great snack and this recipe is quick and easy to prepare. They are crunchy, lightly spicy and tangy and are a seriously addictive snack. Nice eaten hot or cold, it's best you stick to just ¼ cup of these as any more may overload you in terms of energy. I put them into small containers so that I stick roughly to this amount. The ¼ cup of these pepitas really fills you up and keeps you full for a long time.

- **1 ½ cups pumpkin seeds**
- **3 teaspoons unrefined coconut oil**
- **2 teaspoons sweet paprika**
- **3 teaspoons lime juice**
- **2 pinches cayenne pepper**
- **¾ teaspoon Celtic sea salt**

Preheat the oven to 180°C fan forced. Line a large baking tray with baking paper and spread the pumpkin seeds out on the tray. Roast for 15 minutes.

Place the hot pumpkin seeds into a large bowl and add the coconut oil and stir. Add the sweet paprika, lime juice, cayenne and sea salt and stir until well combined.

Dips with Celery Sticks or Rice Crackers

Not a recipe, just a suggestion. Either my *Eggplant Dip*, *Margaret's Hummus*, or *Avocado Dip with Garlic and Chilli* (pages 34–36) served with celery sticks of just a few rice crackers. Celery is a vegetable that contains potassium, a lot of water and celery requires more energy to break it down than it actually gives us so it makes a high nutrient, hydrating, low energy and metabolism boosting snack that is great for weight loss. Alternatively pair with plain rice crackers which are gluten-free and delicious with dips, but don't have too many!

Baked Turmeric Taro Chips

When you start making your own snacks rather than buying them you realise how much you pay for snacks that contain a lot of fat and most often, a lot of colours and preservatives. Taro root is extremely good for you as it is a vegetable that is full of nutrients and fibre. These baked chips make a good, healthy alternative to potato chips and are a great way to get anti-inflammatory turmeric into your diet.

250 g taro root, peeled
1 tablespoon unrefined coconut oil
½ teaspoon sea salt
¼ teaspoon sweet paprika
¼ teaspoon turmeric
Pinch cayenne pepper

Preheat the oven to 200°C fan forced. Line two oven trays with baking paper.

Slice the taro root using a mandolin on the finest setting; you want them nice and thin, approximately 2 mm.

Prepare the salt, sweet paprika, turmeric and cayenne in a bowl and mix well.

Put the coconut oil in a bowl and place it in the hot oven for a couple of minutes to melt.

Put the taro on the lined baking trays and lightly brush each side with the melted coconut oil.

Sprinkle the spice mix with your fingers on the top of the taro pieces and place in the hot oven. Cook for 12 minutes in total but turn the taro pieces over to cook on the other side after 6 minutes.

Tip: Very nice served with Margaret's Hummus on page 34.

SIDE DISHES

Italian Style Silverbeet and Beans

Silverbeet is often the unsung hero when it comes to superfoods. It is high in nutrients, especially iron and folate, high in fibre and it is virtually fat free. It's easy to grow, not overly expensive and a serving of this dish is an instant hit of iron. The silverbeet in this recipe can also be substituted for spinach, but I prefer silverbeet, as the white stalks are particularly tasty. Regular silverbeet is great in this dish but you can also use rainbow chard, a multi-coloured relative of beetroot and silverbeet, which is just as nutrient rich and has sweet tasting yellow, red, orange, purple and white stalks. This side dish is great as lunch the next day with a can of tuna and rice or quinoa.

- 1 large bunch of silverbeet or rainbow chard
- 1 large clove garlic, finely grated
- 400 g can borlotti beans (drained and rinsed)
- Extra virgin olive oil to drizzle
- Celtic sea salt and pepper to taste

Wash and chop the silverbeet or rainbow chard into 1 cm slices. Blanch in a large pot with a couple of inches of water until it wilts down. Drain off most of the water but leave a little water in the pot to keep the dish juicy. Add the grated garlic and the borlotti beans. Drizzle a little olive oil into the dish. Stir and season with salt and pepper.

Serve as a side dish with a little sweet chilli sauce if you wish.

SERVES 4

Ratatouille

This is an excellent side dish as it is full of antioxidants and very tasty. Apart from the initial chopping prep work, there is little more to do except leave it to bubble away. You can really play around with this dish a lot, I add the mushrooms as I find they really make it tasty. It is great as leftovers for lunch the next day and is also very tasty alongside poached eggs for breakfast.

1 medium onion, thinly sliced
1 small to medium eggplant, thinly sliced
5 small mushrooms, thinly sliced
½ green capsicum, diced
½ red capsicum, diced
4 medium fresh tomatoes, diced, or
    1 x 400 g can tinned diced tomatoes
1 medium zucchini, thinly sliced
5 cloves garlic, finely chopped
1 handful fresh basil, torn
Celtic sea salt and cracked pepper

Put all the chopped vegetables in a medium dry pan (no need for any oil) along with ½ the chopped garlic and ¾ of the fresh torn basil. Bring to a simmer and then put the lid on and simmer gently for half an hour or more, stirring occasionally. Remove from the heat and add the rest of the garlic, stir and season with Celtic sea salt and cracked pepper. Add the remaining basil on top as a garnish and serve.

SERVES 6

Roasted Beetroot with Balsamic, Cumin and Yoghurt

Roasted Beetroot With Balsamic, Cumin and Yoghurt

This side dish always impresses with its tangy taste and its bright pink colour! Beetroot is full of iron and folate and is believed to have cancer preventative and anti-inflammatory properties. Also a source of bowel protective fibre and many other nutrients, it is a must have vegetable in an anti-inflammatory diet. Combined with the balsamic vinegar, cumin and yoghurt, this is a tangy and creamy high nutrient anti-inflammatory dish. Great as a leftover (if there is any left) with a simple salad and a can of tuna.

- 6 beetroots, medium to large, peeled
- Extra-virgin olive oil
- Balsamic vinegar
- Maldon salt
- 3 heaped tablespoons Greek yoghurt
- 1 heaped teaspoon cumin, ground
- ½ lemon, juiced
- Sea salt and pepper to taste

Preheat the oven to 190°C.

Peel beetroots (best to wear kitchen gloves!) and cut into large chunks. Smaller beetroots can be cut in half, larger ones will need to be cut into four pieces. Don't cut them too small, as they will dry up too much as they cook.

Place the beetroots into a small oven tray. Drizzle olive oil onto the beetroots, just enough to coat, turning the beetroots so all surfaces are covered. Now drizzle a generous amount of balsamic vinegar onto the beetroots, turning as you go so that all the beetroots are well covered. Put a pinch of Maldon salt on each piece of beetroot, you will also need to be generous with the salt.

Cook for approximately 1.5 hours, turning the beetroots once or twice during cooking. Check they are cooked through before removing them from the oven.

Leave to sit for 5-10 minutes to cool a little. Transfer the beetroots to a serving dish and add the yoghurt, cumin, sea salt and pepper, and lemon juice to taste. Garnish with microgreens if you have them.

SERVES 6

Turmeric and Saffron Rice

This turmeric and saffron rice recipe tastes delicious and it is a quick and easy way to add anti-inflammatory herbs into your diet. Saffron and turmeric are both powerful anti-inflammatory herbs and both also have the added benefic of improving your mood. Saffron is expensive but you don't need a lot here, just make sure you buy good quality saffron in order to ensure the health benefits. You can make this with just the turmeric, but the saffron gives it more of a fragrant flavor. I add black pepper in this recipe because black pepper optimises the absorption of turmeric. As well as being delicious, the rice looks great with its vibrant yellow colour.

- 2 cups basmati or jasmine rice
- 1 teaspoon turmeric powder (or 1 tablespoon grated fresh turmeric)
- ½ teaspoon Celtic sea salt
- Pinch of ground black pepper
- Pinch of saffron (approximately 6 strands)

Can be cooked either on the stovetop or in a rice cooker. If cooking on a stovetop, bring 4 cups of water to a boil and add all the ingredients and stir before covering. Reduce heat to low and simmer until the water is absorbed and rice is cooked, about 20 minutes. If using a rice cooker just add 2½ cups of water and all the ingredients and stir before closing the lid. When rice is cooked, fluff with a fork.

SERVES 4-6

Note: Basmati rice has slightly less carb content than jasmine rice so I tend to use this. This recipe can also be made with brown rice of course, and is equally as delicious.

Spinach and Chinese Mushrooms

Chinese mushrooms are incredibly good for your immune system and are full of nutrients. The spinach in this recipe boosts the nutrients as well. This is a quick and tasty side dish.

- 1 teaspoon refined coconut oil
- 1 clove garlic, finely grated
- 100 g shiitake mushrooms, sliced
- 150 g oyster mushrooms, sliced
- 3 large handfuls baby spinach leaves
- Sea salt and pepper to taste
- 1 teaspoon white sesame seeds (or black if you prefer)

Add the coconut oil to a hot pan and cook the garlic and mushrooms until they are soft. Toss in the spinach leaves and season well with sea salt and pepper to taste. Garnish with white sesame seeds. Turn off immediately and serve.

SERVES 4

Balsamic and Thyme Brussels Sprouts

Brussels sprouts are also part of the *Brassica* family and are incredibly good for you. Anti-inflammatory, good for the liver, and full of nutrients, brussels sprouts tick all the boxes. They are great just steamed on their own, but I also like to make this very tasty side dish for a change.

- 12 Brussels sprouts, trimmed and halved
- 1 teaspoon dried thyme or 3 teaspoons fresh thyme
- 1 teaspoon extra virgin olive oil
- 2 teaspoons balsamic vinegar
- Sea salt and pepper to taste

Steam the Brussels sprouts until bright green and just tender (approximately 6 minutes). Place in a bowl and add the thyme, olive oil and balsamic vinegar, and season with salt and pepper. Toss and serve immediately.

SERVES 4

Roasted Radicchio with Rocket, Balsamic and Goat's Cheese

Roasted Radicchio with Rocket, Balsamic and Goat's Cheese

Radicchio is a wonderful bitter leafy vegetable which is part of the *Chicory* family and is often called Italian chicory. Bitter salad leaves are very good for you as bitters stimulate the digestive tract to produce digestive acids, and therefore they will help your body's digestion of the meal. Radicchio is a very good source of iron and vitamin C. This dish has an unusual flavour combination, tangy, bitter and creamy all at once. We mainly see the round head variety of radicchio which works well in this recipe, but if you come across the long, finger shaped raddichio called Treviso radicchio it has a milder flavour and is excellent roasted.

- 1 large head of radicchio
- Extra virgin olive oil (for drizzling)
- 1 tablespoon chopped fresh thyme, or 1 teaspoon dried
- Sea salt and ground pepper
- Balsamic vinegar (for drizzling)
- 1 large handful rocket
- 100 g goat's cheese

Preheat the oven to 200°C. Rinse the radicchio and slice in half and then cut each half into three wedges. Shake off excess water and place in a small baking tray. Drizzle with a small amount olive oil and add the thyme and sea salt and ground pepper. Toss to coat.

Roast until wilted, approximately 20 minutes.

Remove from the oven and place the roasted radicchio into a medium serving dish. Drizzle with balsamic vinegar and toss to coat. Add the rocket and goats cheese. Serve immediately.

SERVES 6

Dijon, Balsamic and Basil Potatoes

Dijon, Balsamic and Basil Potatoes

This is a tangy and very flavoursome side dish. Potatoes tend to get a bad rap but they contain a lot of phytonutrients such as high levels of potassium and are good to include in your diet once in a while. Growing your own potatoes is easy and fun and they taste incredible in this dish, but if not, store-bought potatoes are fine. This is a good side dish for a BBQ, or for guests as well as a regular night at home. Either way, balance the energy in this dish with a super healthy salad.

- 8 medium sized dutch cream or nicola potatoes, or 16 baby potatoes (these are best but any potato will do)
- 1 tablespoon Dijon mustard
- 1 tablespoon balsamic vinegar
- 1 clove garlic, finely grated
- 1 tablespoon extra virgin olive oil
- ½ lemon, juiced
- 1 small handful fresh parsley, chopped finely
- 1 small handful fresh basil, chopped finely
- Sea salt and pepper to taste

Peel and cut the potatoes into large chunks. Boil the potatoes until cooked, approximately 30 – 40 minutes. Strain and leave in the pot to cool for 5 minutes. Add all the other ingredients including the salt and pepper to taste, and stir. Cover until ready to serve, best served warm.

SERVES 6

Ginger and Garlic Gai Lan

Ginger and Garlic Gai Lan

Gai Lan, otherwise known as Chinese broccoli, is one of many different varieties of broccoli. Broccoli is extremely good for you with its anti-inflammatory properties and this variety is no exception. A member of the *Brassica* family, broccoli is also very good for the liver, is high in nutrients and is considered to be cancer preventative. This dish combines crunchy broccoli stalks with the flavour of the sauce and it makes a great side dish.

3 drops sesame oil
2 bunches gai lan (Chinese broccoli)
2 tablespoons tamari
2 tablespoons oyster sauce
3 drops fish sauce
1 cm piece ginger, peeled and grated
1 clove garlic, grated
Sea salt and pepper to taste
White sesame seeds

Cut the broccoli with the leaves left on into pieces approximately 8 cm long. Combine the tamari, oyster sauce, fish sauce and ginger and garlic in a small bowl and stir until combined. Place the sesame oil in a hot pan and then add the broccoli and cook, stirring for 1 minute. Then add the prepared sauce and cook for another minute, stirring. Season with salt and pepper, stir and place in a serving dish. Sprinkle with the white sesame seeds.

SERVES 4

SALADS

Radicchio Salad

Radicchio Salad

Radicchio is a wonderful bitter leafy vegetable which is part of the *Chicory* family and is often called Italian chicory. As mentioned previously, bitter salad leaves are very good for you as bitters stimulate the digestive tract to produce digestive acids, and therefore they will help your body's digestion of the meal. Radicchio is a very good source of iron and vitamin C. The dressing in this salad is tangy and slightly sweet which balances out the bitterness of the radicchio and the rocket adds a peppery flavour. As well as being very tasty, this salad takes just minutes to make.

½ a large head of radicchio or a whole head if it is small
1 handful rocket

Dressing:
1 tablespoon extra virgin olive oil
1 tablespoon Dijon mustard
½ lemon
1 teaspoon honey
Sea salt and pepper to taste

Place the radicchio in a salad bowl. Add the rocket, pour the dressing into the bowl and toss to combine.

SERVES 4

Tip: Once washed and dried radicchio stores very well in the fridge for 5 days in an airtight bag. This way you can have it on hand and ready to use not just in this salad but in any salad.

Slaw

Cabbage is incredibly good for you with its anti-inflammatory properties and high calcium content. The addition of coriander here further boosts the health properties as it helps to remove heavy metals from the body and adds to the taste of the slaw. This salad goes well with *Rocky's Slow Cooker Pulled Pork* on page 79 or else alongside any dish. Works well as a leftover for lunch the next day as it keeps well.

½ green cabbage, shredded
1 medium carrot, julienned
4 spring onions, finely sliced
1 small handful coriander, chopped
1 lemon, juiced
1 tablespoon flax oil
Sea salt and pepper to taste

Combine all ingredients together in a medium bowl and toss before serving.

SERVES 6

Baby Spinach and Capsicum Salad

This is a light and tasty salad which is full of nutrients.

3 large handfuls baby spinach leaves
¼ medium red onion, thinly sliced in half-moon crescents
½ large green capsicum, chopped

Dressing:
1 ½ teaspoons flaxseed oil
3 teaspoons lemon juice
Sea salt and pepper to taste

Combine in a medium salad bowl and toss before serving.

SERVES 4

Anti-Inflammatory Recipes

Tangy Beetroot Salad

Tangy Beetroot Salad

Raw beetroot is incredibly good for you and doesn't need much embellishment to taste good. It's a great way to get a hit of iron, as well as many other nutrients and it is believed to be another cancer preventative vegetable. Adding goats cheese is optional in this recipe, it certainly doesn't need it but it adds a 'treat' factor and really makes it delicious. Make sure to put on disposable gloves before dealing with the beetroots (unless you want purple hands!) and if you have a julienne slicer it makes quick work of turning the beetroot into pretty matchsticks. This salad goes very well in a Buddha bowl (mentioned on page 36), adding a beautiful purple colour to the dish.

3 medium beetroots, peeled and finely julienned
2 tablespoons extra virgin olive oil
1 lemon, juiced
Sea salt and pepper to taste
100 g goats cheese, crumbled

Combine all ingredients in a medium bowl saving a little goats cheese to add on top for decoration. Add the lemon juice slowly as you may not need it all and don't season with too much salt as the goats cheese is already salty. Decorate with the remaining goats cheese and garnish with microgreens if you have them.

SERVES 6

Fennel and Radish Salad

Fennel and radish are two more vegetables that are highly alkaline. Add the young fennel tops if you have them as they are full of anti-inflammatory nutrients. This salad is fresh and light and the fennel and radish complement each other well.

1 bunch radishes, approximately 6-8 small radishes, julienned into matchsticks
1 medium fennel, julienned into matchsticks, save the fine green tops
2 tablespoons lemon juice
1 tablespoon extra virgin olive oil
Sea Salt and pepper to taste

Combine in a medium bowl including the chopped fine green fennel tops and toss before serving.

SERVES 6

Anti-Inflammatory Recipes

Quinoa Tabouleh

I am calling this a salad but it is equally a side dish. Tabouleh is a great way to get loads of iron and folate into your diet and I find that these are two minerals that a lot of people are deficient in. It's also full of antioxidants that we all need to reduce inflammation and oxidative stress or ageing. Swap the burghul wheat for quinoa and suddenly you have a high protein dish that is gluten-free and full of fibre and nutrients. It's great in a mezze or as a side dish but then you can add a can of tuna or some poached chicken or turkey to it the next day for lunch. It lasts well for three days in the fridge.

- 1 cup uncooked quinoa (see how to cook page 98)
- 2 large bunches flat leaf parsley, finely chopped
- 1 medium bunch mint, finely chopped
- 2 medium tomatoes, cut into small pieces
- 1 small red onion, finely chopped
- 2 lemons, juiced
- 40 ml extra virgin olive oil
- Celtic sea salt and pepper to taste

Cook the quinoa as per instructions on page 98. Allow to cool.

Add the quinoa to a large bowl along with the chopped parsley, mint, tomatoes and onion. Season with salt and pepper, stir in lemon juice and oil and toss to combine.

SERVES 6

Simple Zucchini Salad

I first discovered raw zucchini tastes great in a salad when I had a few too many zucchinis in my garden and was trying different things with them. I tend to pick my zucchinis when they are small, before they get too watery, and if you don't have homegrown zucchinis just pick ones that are a little smaller. Zucchini is full of nutrients and anti-inflammatory properties and by not cooking it here you will retain the maximum amount of nutrients. The zing of the lemon in this recipe takes the zucchini up a level in this simple but very fresh tasting salad. It only takes minutes to make but it is important that you use a vegetable peeler to slice the zucchini lengthways into thin ribbons as this adds to the taste.

2 small zucchinis with the ends chopped off and sliced lengthways with a vegetable peeler into thin ribbons
1 tablespoon extra virgin olive oil
2 tablespoons lemon
Celtic sea salt and pepper to taste

Combine in a medium bowl and toss before serving.

SERVES 6

Red Cabbage Salad

Cabbage is part of the *Brassica* family and as well as being high in anti-inflammatory antioxidants it is believed to have cancer preventative properties. Cabbage is traditionally very good for prevention and treatment of ulceration in the stomach, so great for those suffering from acid reflux. Use either red cabbage or green for this recipe, both taste great and it works well for lunch the next day.

½ red cabbage, finely sliced
1 small handful parsley, chopped finely
½ lemon, juiced
1 teaspoon extra virgin olive oil
Celtic sea salt and pepper to taste

Combine in a medium bowl and enjoy.

SERVES 6

Green Papaya Salad

Green Papaya Salad

This is my take on green papaya salad, a traditional Thai dish. Green papaya is full of digestive enzymes, those that particularly help with the digestion of protein, and it is therefore very good for those with a sluggish digestion. The gut is the key to many things in the body and you are what you eat and actually digest, so any food that helps you to digest is brilliant in my book. Green papaya also has antiseptic properties and therefore helps to balance the gut microbiome by promoting a gut enviroment which allows good bacteria to thrive and is not conducive to undesirable bacteria, viruses, fungus and parasites. This is a crunchy salad which is slightly sweet and sour and it is full of nutrients. If you don't like chilli just leave it out. This salad keeps really well in the fridge and works well as leftovers the next day. You will find the green papya at an Asian grocery.

- 1 small green papaya 500 g, peeled and seeded
- 10 cherry tomatoes, halved or 1 small tomatoe cut into small chunks
- 15 green beans cut into 3 cm pieces
- Small handful each of Thai basil or regular basil, Vietnamese mint, mint and coriander leaves (don't slice, use the whole leaves with no stem)

Dressing:
- 2 tablespoons fish sauce
- 2 tablespoons apple cider vinegar
- 1 tablespoon lime juice
- 2 tablespoons honey
- ½ cup water
- 1 large clove garlic, chopped finely
- 1 chilli, seeded and chopped finely
- 1 tablespoon crushed roasted cashews to garnish
- 1 chilli, seeded and sliced thinly to garnish

To make the dressing, combine all ingredients in a bowl and whisk until the honey disolves. Set aside.

Use a mandolin or a julienne peeler to shred the green papaya into fine matchsticks. Add the green papaya to a large bowl along with the tomatoes, beans and herbs. Finally, add the dressing to taste, (I generally add about 10 tablespoons). Toss and garnish with the crushed cashews and sliced chilli.

SERVES 6

Lentil Salad

This is great to make as a salad to have with dinner and then it works well as lunch the next day. It contains protein and fibre and lots of nutrients but most importantly it is very tasty. Feel free to play around with the vegetables you use in this salad. I find this combination works well, but any salad vegetables you have in the fridge would work as the lentils lend themselves to many flavors.

- 2 cans organic or regular lentils, drained and rinsed (if you have time use lentils you have soaked and cooked yourself)
- ¼ red onion, diced into small pieces
- 2 mushrooms, diced into small pieces
- 1 Lebanese cucumber, diced into small pieces
- 1 medium tomato, diced into small pieces
- ½ red capsicum, diced into small pieces
- 1 stick celery including any young green tops, diced into small pieces
- A handful of salad leaves such as rocket, spinach leaves, watercress, curly endive, witloof, chickory, or oakleaf lettuce
- 1 large handful fresh herbs such as parsley, dill, basil, mint, Vietnamese mint, chives, tarragon, any or all of these if you have them

Dressing:
1 tablespoon extra virgin olive oil
2 tablespoons lemon juice
Celtic sea salt and pepper to taste

Combine in a medium bowl and enjoy.

SERVES 6

Tip: For variety substitute the lentils for cannellini beans, chickpeas or butter beans.

Tasty Green Salad

This is my 'go-to' salad as it is full of anti-inflammatory herbs and vegetables and is very tasty. I add a big handful of herbs from my garden and I'd really encourage you to grow your own, but if not, it is worth buying fresh herbs as they are full of anti-inflammatory nutrients and they really make the difference in taste to this salad. I also add a raw clove of garlic which I finely dice. When garlic is raw its health properties are more potent and it has many health benefits including boosting the immune system, improving heart health and cholesterol levels, and protecting the body against heavy metals. Some people unfortunately can't have garlic due to FODMAP issues, but if you are able to have it you will find it tastes great in a salad.

1 large Lebanese cucumber
1 small carrot
3 button mushrooms
½ red capsicum
1 medium tomato
1 stick celery including any young green tops
3 spring onions including the green tops, or small amount of red onion
½ avocado
1 handful fresh herbs such as mint, tarragon, basil, parsley
1 clove garlic, finely diced
1 mignonette lettuce (or any salad greens such as rocket, spinach leaves, radicchio, watercress)

Dressing:
2 ½ tablespoons apple cider vinegar
1 ½ tablespoons seeded mustard
1 ½ tablespoons flaxseed oil
Sea salt and pepper to taste

Combine in a large salad bowl and toss before serving.

SERVES 6

SOUP

Roasted Cauliflower, Cumin and Ginger Chicken Soup

It's the roasted cauliflower, cumin and ginger that make the difference in this flavorsome soup. Once you roast cauliflower, its taste completely changes and it is a supreme anti-inflammatory vegetable. Serve this on its own or add carbs such as brown rice, quinoa or noodles if you wish.

- 1 teaspoon refined coconut oil
- 4 large cloves garlic, grated
- 1 leek washed well and thinly sliced
- 3 sticks celery, finely diced
- 1 large carrot, finely diced
- 7 medium mushrooms, finely diced
- 1 kg free range and organic skinless chicken thigh fillets
- ½ large cauliflower, chopped to small to medium pieces
- Extra virgin olive oil to drizzle
- 2 heaped teaspoons cumin, ground
- 3 cm knob ginger, peeled and grated
- 2 heaped teaspoons dried tarragon
- Celtic sea salt
- Cracked pepper

Heat the coconut oil in a large heavy-based saucepan over medium heat. Add half the garlic and the leek, celery and carrot and sweat down stirring frequently. Turn the heat down a little and add the mushrooms, stirring for a minute. Add the chicken and cook, stirring, for five minutes.

Meanwhile turn the oven to 200°C fan forced. Take a tray lined with baking paper and place the cauliflower on it. Drizzle olive oil over the cauliflower and shake the cumin on top. Gently toss to combine and place in the oven to cook for approximately 30 minutes.

Add the ginger, tarragon, and the rest of the garlic to the cooking chicken and vegetable mixture and season well with salt and pepper. Cook for a minute, stirring and then add boiled water to the mixture until just covered. Turn the heat up and bring to a simmer. Once simmering, turn the heat to low and place the lid on. Cook for 1 hour or more. Add the cooked cauliflower to the pot when ready and continue cooking in with the soup.

After the soup has been cooking for an hour or so, remove the lid and turn the heat up for a further 10 minutes to allow it to thicken before serving.

Serve on its own or on a bed of quinoa, brown rice, soba noodles, or small pasta for kids.

SERVES 4 (as a standalone soup) and will stretch further if carbs are added

Watercress Soup

Watercress is incredibly good for you but doesn't seem to make the list of superfoods too often. Another member of the hailed *Brassica* family, it too is full of nutrients, especially vitamin K, which is crucial for bone health. Believed to have cancer preventative properties and containing very little fat or carbohydrates it is often considered to enhance detox and weight loss. This soup is very tasty as watercress has a peppery, spiciness to it and the soup looks impressive with its vibrant green colour. It is also quick to make. Watercress can be found at supermarkets these days, or else at organic or general greengrocers, but I tend to pick up the large quantity needed for this soup at an Asian greengrocer.

- 1 teaspoon unrefined coconut oil
- 2 medium potatoes, diced small
- 1 medium onion, chopped roughly
- 2 cloves garlic, chopped roughly
- 3 bunches watercress, clean well and remove any large stems, chop roughly
- Celtic sea salt and pepper to taste

Heat the coconut oil and then sweat the potatoes, onion and garlic by stirring for a few minutes. Add 700 mls (boiling) water and simmer until potato is soft (about 15- 20 minutes).

Add the watercress and simmer for 3- 4 minutes. Turn off the heat. Using a hand blender, liquidise until smooth.

SERVES 2 as a meal, or SERVES 4 as an entrée

Tip: I have served this up as an entrée at a dinner party in small bowls with a swirl of cream added at the end for a treat, it really impressed, and started the dinner off in a healthy way.

Coconut and Spinach Dahl

Coconut and Spinach Dahl

Lentils are a great source of protein and when you add iron rich spinach and fragrant herbs you get a really anti-inflammatory effect from this soup. It takes about an hour to cook from start to finish and you can either serve it alone or with rice and yoghurt. This recipe is creamy and flavoursome, just remove the chilli flakes if you don't like it too spicy.

- 1 tablespoon unrefined coconut oil
- 1 large red onion, finely chopped
- 1 stick celery, chopped finely, including any green tops
- 3 cm fresh ginger, peeled and finely grated
- 2 large cloves garlic, finely grated
- 2 bay leaves
- 1 cinnamon stick
- 3 cm fresh turmeric, finely grated, or 2 teaspoons dried turmeric
- 1 teaspoon cumin
- ½ teaspoon garam masala
- ½ teaspoon chilli flakes
- 1 ½ cups dried red lentils (you can also use French style lentils, these are darker and nuttier)
- 3 ½ cups vegetable stock (home made if possible)
- 1 cup light coconut milk
- 2 large handfuls baby spinach leaves, chopped roughly
- 1 ½ teaspoons Celtic sea salt
- Few shakes of pepper
- 2 tablespoons lemon juice
- Large handful coriander, to garnish

Use a medium-sized heavy-based pot and put it on medium to low heat. Add the coconut oil, onion and celery and stir for 2 minutes. Add the ginger and garlic and stir, followed by the bay leaves, cinnamon stick, turmeric, cumin, garam masala and chilli flakes. Stir for a couple of minutes until fragrant and then add the lentils, vegetable stock and coconut milk. Turn up the heat to bring to a boil and then turn down to simmer, covered for 40 minutes. Add the chopped spinach and the salt and pepper and cook for 5 minutes with the lid on. The dahl should be thick and creamy, if not cook a little longer. Fish out the bay leaves and cinnamon stick and add the lemon juice before serving.

Garnish with coriander and serve as a standalone soup or else serve with basmati or brown rice and yoghurt.

SERVES 4 as an entrée sized soup or SERVES 4 with rice and yoghurt as a dinner

DINNER

Poached Salmon with Soba Noodles and Black Sesame

One of the healthiest ways to cook salmon is to poach it. It is also fairly quick and you can be preparing the side dishes while it bubbles away. Salmon is a large oily fish and therefore contains higher levels of mercury so be careful not to have it more than once per week. Wild salmon is better for you if you can get your hands on it.

500 – 600 g salmon fillets
Celtic sea salt and cracked pepper
1 tablespoon Dijon mustard
1 large clove garlic finely chopped
2 cm knob finely chopped ginger
1 small handful fresh chopped herbs such as coriander, chives, Vietnamese mint, thyme, thai basil, tarragon (I use whatever I have in the garden - use dried herbs if you don't have fresh)
1 lemon
Black sesame seeds to garnish
270 g packet organic soba noodles
Tamari to drizzle on the soba noodles
Coriander to garnish (optional)

Rinse the salmon and put it into a frying pan and fill with water ¾ way up the fish. Lightly season the fish with sea salt and freshly ground pepper. Apply the Dijon mustard on top of the salmon and use a spoon to spread it all over each piece. Sprinkle the garlic, ginger and chopped herbs on top of the Dijon mustard. Squeeze the juice of half the lemon on top of the fish and cut the other half into slices and drop into the water. Put a lid on the pan.

Meanwhile bring a pot of water to the boil and cook the soba noodles in rapid boiling water for approximately 4 minutes then drain. Put back into the pot and drizzle the noodles with tamari.

Cook the salmon for approximately 15-20 minutes on low heat. Don't remove the lid at all during cooking. Check it is cooked through before removing from the pan (it should be just pink) and place on top of a serving of soba noodles. Garnish both the noodles and salmon with black sesame seeds. Squeeze a little lemon or lime juice on the salmon before serving and a little fresh coriander if you have it. Goes well with any of my side dishes or salads but especially *Italian Style Silverbeet and Beans* on page 42 or *Ginger and Garlic Gai Lan* on page 53.

SERVES 4

Vegetarian Eggplant Curry

This vegetarian dish doesn't take long to make and it keeps well as a leftover for lunch the next day. Eggplants are a wonderful vegetable as they are full of nutrients (many of which are in the skin so don't cut it off), low in calories, high in fibre, and contain no fat. I have converted a few friends who don't like vegetarian food with this dish as it is so tasty and it is also one of my children's favourite dinners! If you serve it with some yoghurt on top you balance the dish by adding the protein in the yoghurt (it also tastes great with the yoghurt but it certainly doesn't have to have it, it is lovely without).

- 1 teaspoon refined coconut oil
- 1 onion, diced into 1 cm pieces
- 2 large eggplants, diced into 2 cm cubes
- 1 tablespoon of Celtic sea salt
- ½ teaspoon pepper
- 3 tablespoons 'Clive of India' or alternate brand curry powder
- 2 teaspoons garam masala
- 2 teaspoons cumin, ground
- ½ teaspoon chilli powder (this is for a mild curry, increase for a hotter curry)
- ½ teaspoon turmeric powder or 3 cm piece fresh turmeric root peeled and finely grated
- 2 x 400 g cans of diced peeled tomatoes

Optional: serve with a dollop of Greek yoghurt or plain low fat yoghurt

Heat the coconut oil in a large deep frying pan over medium heat. Lightly fry the onion and eggplants and add the salt and pepper. When the eggplant appears almost cooked thoroughly mix in the curry powder, garam masala, cumin, chilli and turmeric. Add in the cans of diced tomatoes and bring to the boil, cover and simmer for about 20-30 minutes. Serve on a bed of either basmati rice, brown rice, wild rice with basmati or quinoa and a dollop of Greek yoghurt or low fat yoghurt on top if you wish.

SERVES 4-6

Land and Sea Paella

Land and Sea Paella

After a recent trip to Barcelona where we fell in love with paella, this dish has become one of our family favourites. With saffron, paprika, fresh tomatoes, garlic, fresh seafood, green beans and parsley it is a delicious anti-inflammatory dish. This Land and Sea Paella is mainly seafood but there is a small amount of chicken and pork as I find it improves the flavor. It is not the cheapest dinner to make but I think it is worth it. Many people don't attempt cooking paella because they think it is too hard to make but this is a surprisingly simple and quick method and it will definitely impress. You can invest in a paella pan but not essential, I make this in a large, wide fry pan.

- 4 cups chicken stock
- 2 cups water
- ½ teaspoon saffron threads
- 2 teaspoons refined coconut oil
- 1 red onion, finely chopped
- 2 garlic cloves, crushed
- 2 cups arborio rice (or bomba rice, traditional Spanish paella rice, if you can get it)
- 2 tomatoes, diced
- 2 teaspoons smoked paprika
- Celtic sea salt and pepper
- 1 skinless chicken thigh, cut into 3 x 1 cm strips
- 1 pork butterfly steak, cut into 3 x 1 cm strips
- 250 g fish fillets (such as orange roughy), cut into 3 x 1 cm strips
- 12 medium king prawns, peeled
- 12 mussels, scrubbed, debearded
- 12 pipis
- Small handful of green beans
- Small handful of chopped parsley
- 4 lemon wedges

Combine stock, water and saffron in a medium saucepan and bring to a boil. Cover and reduce heat to low, keeping it at a simmer. Using a large, wide fry pan over medium to high heat, add 1 of the teaspoons of coconut oil and cook the onion and garlic until soft. Once softened, add the rice, diced tomatoes, smoked paprika and gently season with salt and pepper. Stir the mixture to ensure an even coating over the rice. Add half the stock mixture to the frying pan and bring to the boil using a medium to high heat, then reduce heat to medium. Leave the pan covered and cook for around 15-20 minutes or until stock is absorbed, mixing every few minutes. Meanwhile, in a separate pan, fry the chicken and pork with the second teaspoon of coconut oil on high heat and add a sprinkling of salt and pepper. Cook for a few minutes until just cooked. Mix the chicken and pork into the rice mixture as well as the fish. Next place the mussels around the pan pressing gently into the rice mixture. Add half the remaining stock mixture and cook covered until the liquid is absorbed. Add beans, prawns and pipis pressing gently into rice mixture. Add the last of the stock and cook covered until liquid is almost absorbed (5 to 10 minutes) to allow the crust to form on the bottom of the pan. Turn off the heat and let sit, covered for 5 minutes. Garnish with chopped parsley and lemon wedges.

SERVES 4

Rocky's Slow Cooker Pulled Pork

Rocky's Slow Cooker Pulled Pork

My pulled pork is easy to make and full of flavor. I consider this dish more of a treat, perfect for guests or for special weekend dinners. Pork is a red meat even though it is marketed as a 'white meat' and red meat isn't anti-inflammatory so this is one reason why I put this in the treat category. The other reason is that brown rice malt syrup contains sugar (one positive is that it contains virtually no fructose so it is safe for people on the FODMAP diet). I decided to include this dish as it is a much healthier version of traditional pulled pork recipes with the addition of anti-inflammatory herbs and spices, apple cider vinegar, and trimming the fat off the pork at the beginning also helps. It goes perfectly with my *Slaw* on page 57 and this brings it up a notch in health too. If you like your house to smell like heaven while it cooks you will love this. You will need a large 5-6 litre slow cooker for this recipe.

- 2 kg pork shoulder, boneless
- 2 tablespoons smoked paprika
- 2 teaspoons fennel seeds, ground in a mortar and pestle
- 1 teaspoon pepper
- 1 teaspoon cayenne pepper
- 2 teaspoons Celtic sea salt
- 6 large cloves garlic, chopped finely
- 3 tablespoons organic rice malt syrup (made from brown rice)
- ½ cup apple cider vinegar
- ½ cup water
- 2 spring onions including the green tops, sliced thinly
- 5 drops liquid smoke* (optional)
- Handful of fresh coriander to garnish, chopped

Take the time to trim the pork shoulder of as much fat as possible.

Mix together the spice mix by combining the smoked paprika, ground fennel seeds, pepper, cayenne pepper, salt, garlic and rice malt cereal in a bowl until it combines to form a paste. Rub the spice mix into all sides of the pork, concentrating on the top, sides and in between any pieces. Place the vinegar and water into the bottom of the slow cooker. Put the pork into the slow cooker and place the chopped spring onions all over the pork. Keep as much of the garlic, spices and spring onions on the pork as possible. Carefully place 5 drops of the liquid smoke directly onto the pork.

Cover and cook on low in a slow cooker for 8 hours. Turn off the slow cooker and allow the pork to rest, covered, for 10 minutes or so.

Remove the pork and shred using two forks.

Place in a serving bowl adding some of the juices as desired. Garnish with fresh coriander.

Best served with my Slaw on page 57.

SERVES 6-8

*Liquid smoke is available at specialty stores. I picked mine up at a BBQ store. It imparts a smoky flavor without having to put the dish through the smoking process that isn't always healthy. It is not essential for this recipe, but if you can get your hands on it, it does add a beautiful, subtle smoky flavor.

Fragrant Fish Curry

Fragrant Fish Curry

This fragrant fish curry is full of anti-inflammatory herbs, spices and vegetables and is absolutely delicious and quick to make.

- 3 cups basmati rice
- 1 teaspoon unrefined coconut oil
- 2 cm knob fresh ginger, finely chopped
- 2 cloves garlic, finely chopped
- 2 cm piece fresh turmeric, peeled and grated (or 1 teaspoon dried)
- 2 teaspoons cumin, ground
- 2 teaspoons garam masala
- ½ lime
- ¼ red onion thinly sliced
- ½ red capsicum cut into 2 cm thin sticks
- ½ zucchini cut into 2 cm thin sticks
- ½ carrot cut into 2 cm thin sticks
- 200 g tin diced peeled tomatoes
- 250 ml light coconut milk
- 600 g orange roughy or other white fish, cut into 2 cm cubes
- Celtic sea salt and pepper to taste
- 12 snow peas cut into 3 pieces, or 12 green beans
- Fresh coriander and sliced red chilli to garnish

Prepare the rice in a rice cooker or on the stovetop.

Heat the coconut oil in a frypan over medium heat. Add the ginger, garlic, turmeric, cumin, garam masala and lime juice to the pan and cook for 1 minute. Add the red onion, red capsicum, zucchini, carrot and peeled tomatoes and cook for 2 minutes. Reduce the heat and add the coconut milk and the fish. Season with salt and pepper. Bring to a gentle simmer and cook, covered for 10-15 minutes. Add the snow peas/ green beans and turn it off. Garnish with the coriander and sliced chilli.

SERVES 4

Ma Po Tofu with Eggplant and Cauliflower

Ma Po Tofu with Eggplant and Cauliflower

I have taken this popular Chinese dish up a notch in health with the addition of eggplant and cauliflower. Full of herbs and spices it is very tasty and works well for lunch the next day. This dish is so tasty that the four of us usually eat this entire amount. I generally double the recipe so that we have leftovers the next day.

- 1 teaspoon coconut oil, unrefined
- 1 medium red onion, diced
- 500 g pork mince
- 1 eggplant (small to medium), cut into 1 cm cubes
- 3 garlic cloves, grated
- 3 cm knob of fresh ginger, grated
- 3 cm piece of fresh turmeric, grated
- 1 teaspoon Celtic sea salt
- Few shakes pepper
- 3 tablespoons kecap manis
- 1 lime, juiced
- 120 g cauliflower, cut into small pieces
- 300 g silken tofu (GMO free), diced small
- 120 g cherry tomatoes, cut in half
- 1 handful fresh basil
- Fresh red chilli sliced to garnish if you wish

Add the coconut oil to a hot pan and then the onion, pork mince and eggplant and cook on medium heat stirring occasionally for 5 minutes. Once softened, add the garlic, ginger, turmeric and salt and pepper and cook on medium heat, stirring for a further 10 minutes.

Put the lid on, bring to a simmer and then add the kecap manis, and lime juice. Reduce to low heat and simmer covered for approximately 30 minutes.

Add the cauliflower, tofu and tomatoes and turn off. Let it sit for 10 minutes.

Serve with *Turmeric and Saffron Rice* (page 46), brown rice, basmati rice or quinoa.

Garnish when serving with the basil leaves and fresh cut up chilli if you wish.

SERVES 4

San Choy Bau

San Choy Bau

This is my take on the classic San Choy Bau where I replace the traditional pork mince with turkey mince. I have tried it with both and I find the turkey version tastes even better than pork! Turkey is a good form of protein because it is lean and is high in tryptophan, a wonderful protein that helps produce serotonin, the chemical that makes us happy. Turkey is also high in selenium and many other minerals and antioxidants. The cauliflower gives a great crunch and adds more nutrients. I like to have some of this in lettuce bowls, but I also prepare bean vermicelli and serve some of the turkey mix with that, just for variety.

- 2 tablespoons tamari
- 4 tablespoons oyster sauce
- 1 teaspoon fish sauce
- 1 lime, juiced
- 1 tablespoon sesame oil
- 1 red onion, finely diced
- 4 cloves garlic, finely grated
- 4 cm piece fresh ginger, peeled and finely grated
- 4 cm piece fresh turmeric, peeled and finely grated
- 1 kg turkey mince
- ½ teaspoon Celtic sea salt
- Few shakes pepper
- 200 g cauliflower chopped into 1 cm pieces
- 250 g bean thread vermicelli (made from pea, mung bean and corn)
- 1 iceberg lettuce, washed and separated, to use as 'bowls'
- 1 fresh chilli to garnish
- Large handful coriander to garnish

Combine the tamari, oyster sauce, fish sauce and lime juice in a small bowl.

Add the sesame oil, onion, garlic, ginger and turmeric to a medium hot pan, cook for one minute. Add the turkey mince and salt and pepper and cook for 5 minutes, stirring.

Turn down the heat a little and add the tamari mixture to the turkey, and cook for 3 minutes.

Add the cauliflower, mix and immediately turn off. Allow to sit covered, for 5 minutes.

Meanwhile cover the vermicelli with boiling water, leave to sit for 10 minutes and then strain.

Prepare your San Choy Bau by placing some in each lettuce cup and garnish each with fresh chilli and coriander. As a side dish, mix some of the turkey mixture with vermicelli, garnish with chilli and coriander and serve in a medium bowl.

SERVES 6

Thai Chicken Curry

Thai Chicken Curry

This is a fragrant curry containing three members of the ginger family: ginger, turmeric and galangal. All three have strong anti-inflammatory and anti-cancer properties. You may not know galangal but it is worth sourcing and it's not hard to find these days. It adds a sharp unusual citrus flavour to dishes. You peel and grate it just as you would ginger or turmeric (it has more of a woody texture). Store galangal in the fridge along with your ginger and turmeric. This curry has the red curry flavour but with the addition of the extra turmeric, ginger, galangal and lemongrass it turns a more yellow colour and this adds to its anti-inflammatory action.

½ teaspoon unrefined coconut oil
1 kg quality free range or organic chicken thighs roughly cut up (or chicken breasts if you prefer)
500 g eggplant cut into 2 cm cubes
Celtic sea salt and pepper
1 clove garlic, grated
3 cm knob galangal root, peeled and finely grated
3 cm knob ginger root, peeled and finely grated
3 cm knob turmeric root, peeled and finely grated
1 stick lemongrass, finely grated
1 medium onion, diced
1 tablespoon Thai red curry paste
400 ml light coconut milk
Small handful of coriander chopped and extra to garnish
3 drops fish sauce
½ lime
1 fresh red chilli, chopped thinly with the seeds removed to garnish

Add the coconut oil to a hot pan and cook chicken for a few minutes on medium heat. Add the eggplant and cook for another few minutes. Add 1 teaspoon sea salt and some cracked pepper.

Add the garlic, galangal, ginger, turmeric and lemongrass and stir until fragrant. Add the onion and Thai red curry paste and cook stirring for 2 minutes.

Turn down the heat and add the coconut milk and the small handful or coriander and leave to gently simmer for half an hour covered.

Add the 3 drops of fish sauce and the juice of half a lime and turn off the heat. Leave to sit for 5 - 10 minutes before serving.

Serve with brown rice, *Turmeric and Saffron Rice* on page 46, basmati rice, or a blend of black rice and basmati.

Garnish with coriander and fresh chilli if you wish before serving.

SERVES 6

Glazed Salmon with Tricolor Quinoa and Black Rice

Glazed Salmon with Tricolor Quinoa and Black Rice

I consider this slightly more of a treat (since the salmon is pan-fried with a tiny amount of sesame oil and the glaze contains sugar in the oyster sauce) but along with the black rice, the tricolor quinoa, and a healthy vegetable side dish, it is balanced out to become a tasty and very healthy meal. Compared to other rice varieties black rice contains more protein, more fibre, the most antioxidants of any rice, and iron as well. Tricolor quinoa is a combination of red, white and black quinoa. It's very tasty and full of complete protein, fibre and nutrients. With this recipe you will most likely have some black rice and quinoa left over for lunch the next day.

½ cup black rice
1 ½ cups water
1 cup tricolor quinoa
2 cups water
1 clove garlic, finely grated
2 cm piece ginger, peeled and finely grated
½ lime, juiced
2 tablespoons tamari
1 tablespoon oyster sauce
500 – 600 g of salmon fillets
Celtic sea salt and pepper
3 drops sesame oil
Black sesame to garnish

Get the black rice on first, as it takes longer to cook. Rinse the black rice 2 to 3 times with cold water. Add the rice and 1 ½ cups cold water to a small saucepan and bring to the boil. Reduce to a simmer and cook covered for 40 minutes. Remove from heat and stand, covered, for 5 – 10 minutes. Drain any water just before serving.

To cook the quinoa, rinse it thoroughly with a fine sieve and add the quinoa along with the 2 cups cold water to a medium saucepan. Bring to a boil, reduce to a simmer and cook covered for 15 – 20 minutes or until the water has been absorbed. Fluff with a fork.

Combine the garlic, ginger, lime juice, tamari and oyster sauce in a small bowl. Season both sides of the salmon with salt and pepper. Add the 3 drops sesame oil to a hot frypan and add the salmon fillets to the pan. Cook on high heat for 3 minutes each side and then pour on the sauce and cook for one further minute.

Remove the salmon, garnish with black sesame, and serve immediately with the tricolor quinoa and black rice mixed together. Serve alongside Asian greens, steamed vegetables or any of my side dishes.

SERVES 4

Tuna Steak with Herb Drizzle

This is a very quick dish to make and the lemony herb drizzle really adds flavor to the tuna.

600 g of tuna steak
½ teaspoon refined coconut oil
Celtic sea salt and pepper to taste

Drizzle:
2 tablespoons of extra virgin olive oil
½ lemon
4 tablespoons fresh chopped herbs (chives, tarragon, parsley, Vietnamese mint, basil or 2 tablespoons dried herbs)
Celtic sea salt and pepper to taste

Add the refined coconut oil to a hot pan. Place the tuna steaks in the pan and sprinkle salt and pepper on top of the steaks. Cook on high for 3 minutes. Turn and cook the other side for another 3 minutes. Remove from the pan and leave to rest on a plate, covered, for 2 minutes.

While the fish cooks, in a small bowl combine the olive oil, lemon, chopped herbs and salt and pepper.

Once the tuna steaks have rested, drizzle the oil mixture on top.

SERVES 4

Tip: The tuna goes well with the Radicchio Salad on page 56.

Lemon Tuna and Noodles with Vegetables and Seaweed

This is a very tasty dish with the addition of the lemon and the seaweed. Seaweed is a good source of iodine and it adds a beautiful flavour. This makes quite a big batch but any leftovers are great for lunch the next day as the flavours improve overnight. There are a lot of anti-inflammatory vegetables in this dish. You could use any vegetables that you have on hand, but I find that this combination of vegetables tastes particularly good.

- 1 large zucchini, halved and thinly sliced
- 3 stalks celery, thinly sliced, including any young green leafy tops
- ½ small cabbage (675 g approximately), thinly sliced
- 8 mushrooms, thinly sliced
- 1 red capsicum, thinly sliced
- 4 cloves garlic, finely chopped or grated
- 3 cm knob of ginger, finely chopped or grated
- 2 x 425 g cans of tuna
- 2 lemons
- 2 sheets nori seaweed
- Herbamare seasoning (a seasoning salt made from herbs and vegetables)
- 450 g organic soba noodles

I use the food processor to slice the vegetables in this dish as it cuts the prep time down a lot. Use a thin blade, as you want the vegetables thin and not too big, the size of the vegetables adds to the look and taste of the dish.

Add the sliced zucchini, celery, cabbage, mushrooms and capsicum to a large pot over medium heat (no need for any oil, just stir a lot and the vegetables will produce juice that keeps them from sticking). Add half of the chopped garlic and all of the ginger. Stir frequently and cook for approximately 25 minutes on medium to low heat, allowing the vegetables to soften.

Meanwhile bring a large pot of water to the boil. Add the noodles and cook as per instructions.

Once the vegetables have softened, add the drained tuna (break up with a knife before adding). Tear the sheets of nori seaweed into strips and cut into small pieces with kitchen scissors and add to the dish.

Drain the noodles and while in the colander chop them with a knife into smaller pieces and add a good few shakes of Herbamare seasoning to taste. Squeeze the lemon onto the noodles and stir the noodles to distribute the flavours. Add the noodles to the vegetable and tuna mixture along with the rest of the garlic, stir and check if more seasoning is required. Garnish with more shredded seaweed if you have it. Turn off the heat and sit covered for 5 minutes before serving.

SERVES 6 - 8

HOME REMEDIES

Acute Lung Tonic

Below is an old remedy for coughs, bronchitis, mucous in the lungs and colds and flu. It is best made before bed as it promotes a better sleep, which in itself can help you to get better. The mixture helps the body to fight the infection as it stimulates circulation and will raise the body temperature (you may find you sweat overnight). It tends to have an expectorant action on the lungs and helps to loosen up any mucous in your chest so that you are able to cough it up. Made from ingredients that we often have in our cupboards, this can be made up easily when the need arises. You should find you wake up feeling somewhat better the next day.

- 1 cup red wine
- 3 slices lemon
- 2 cloves
- 2 slices fresh ginger
- 1 – 2 tablespoons honey

Add red wine, lemon slices, cloves and ginger to a small saucepan and bring to the boil. As soon as it is bubbling turn the heat to low and light a match over the saucepan until the mixture ignites. Be careful! Most of the alcohol is burnt off in this process.

Wait until the flame has dispersed before taking it off the heat. Pour into a mug (strain out the ginger, lemon and cloves pieces) and add the honey before drinking.

Tip: Making this remedy once usually does the trick, but in coughs that are deep set and have been in the lungs for longer, you may need to do this remedy a few times.

Alkaline Potassium Soup

When we have eaten too many acidic and indulgent foods we need to alkalise the body to get our digestion back on track. I find this soup is the easiest way to achieve this.

The soup is high in vitamins, trace minerals (particularly potassium), and natural salts. The vegetables and herbs contained in it are especially alkaline and anti-inflammatory. It is easy to make and feels very soothing in the stomach.

Depending on how much your liver and digestion feel off track, you could just make a pot of soup for dinner one night or you could make a large batch and consume it over a few days.

Another thing to do is to have *Alkaline Potassium Soup* for dinner once per week to give your digestion a rest. If you decide to do this you could always add some chicken to the vegetables and/or serve it with some brown rice or quinoa. It is a great way to 'clean the slate' once per week.

Celery (most important ingredient – lots)
Spinach, silverbeet or rainbow chard
Leek
Carrot
Broccoli
Cabbage
Cauliflower
Mushroom including Chinese mushrooms such as shiitake and oyster
Parsley (lots)
Watercress
Tumeric (2 cm knob, peeled and grated)
Garlic

Cut the vegetables fairly small and put in a pot, cover with water so that it sits a couple of inches above the vegetables. Bring to the boil and then let simmer for about an hour or until the vegetables are soft. Don't add any salt or pepper or condiments.

Traditionally this soup is strained to make a broth but I just can't bring myself to strain off the vegetable matter. Since the vegetables are cooked they are easily digested and throwing out vegetable fibre seems a waste. I prefer this as a soup with the fibre intact, rather than a broth but it's up to you.

Note: Consider whether you want to buy organic vegetables for the soup. If it is possible, it is worthwhile. If not, don't worry, non-organic will be fine.

THINGS YOU SHOULD KNOW...

How to Cook Quinoa

There are many types of quinoa, namely white, red, black, tricolor (which is a pre-mixed blend of white, red and black) and I believe there is also purple and orange but I haven't tried these. White quinoa is the lightest and fluffiest and most easily substitutes for rice while red is nuttier and chewier, and black has a chewier texture also and a slightly sweeter taste. Quinoa is high in protein, fibre and nutrients. The black and the red contain a little more fibre and they also contain more iron. A good starting point with quinoa is to try the white quinoa first but I recommend you give the tricolor a go as well.

Quinoa is fairly quick to cook. Depending on the amounts you are cooking and the type of quinoa, it usually takes around 20 minutes. You will find that being gluten-free, quinoa tends to feel better in your stomach, and because it is higher in fibre and protein it will keep you full for longer. Most importantly, quinoa is delicious and kids like it too!

Thoroughly rinse one part organic or good quality quinoa in a fine sieve (important as this removes quinoa's natural coating, saponin, which can make it taste soapy or bitter).

Place drained quinoa and two parts water in a medium-sized saucepan and bring to the a boil.

Turn the heat right down to low and cook, covered, until all the water is absorbed (approximately 20 minutes).

Fluff with a fork and it is done!

Lasts well in the fridge for 3-4 days

Tip: I tend to cook 1 cup dried quinoa for a small side dish for four and 2 cups dried quinoa when I want a side dish for four and leftovers for lunch as well.

How to Grow Microgreens

Visit any trendy or fine dining restaurant and you will no doubt find yourself eating microgreens. Microgreens are the seedlings of edible vegetables and herbs that are harvested when they are up to 2 inches tall. They are often used as an attractive garnish and as well as making any dish look good they are also full of nutrients. For a tiny plant they pack a punch of flavor as well.

The problem with microgreens is that they are expensive to buy and not easy to find. If you like to grow things you will really enjoy growing microgreens, as they are easy to grow and they can be grown inside. By growing them you will save yourself money and you will always have them on hand to make a dish look and taste better. Most importantly you will be adding another highly nutritious and anti-inflammatory food to your diet.

YOU WILL NEED:

A few tubs such as the containers that mushrooms come in at the supermarket.

Microgreen seeds, which are best bought online. My favourite is amaranth, which is tasty and highly nutritious and adds a fabulous purple colour to a dish. Others to try are radish, mustard and rocket; any really, just give them a go!

In the cooler months they can be grown inside on a sunny windowsill, but in the warmer months they can be grown outside. Alternatively, you can do as I did and buy a growlight so that they can be grown inside all year round.

If the tubs you have chosen don't have holes in them poke a few drainage holes into the bottom. Cover the bottom of the container with an inch or two of good quality organic potting mix which has inbuilt fertilizer. Use a spray bottle with water to wet the soil a little. Place a scattering of the microgreen seeds, they can be fairly thickly scattered. Place a thin layer of potting mix on top of the seeds. Pat down with your hand and dampen the soil with a few sprays from the spray bottle. Place in a sunny windowsill in winter or else outside in the warmer months. Spray with water 2-3 times a day if you can, especially in the first few days.

The microgreens will start to emerge after 3 – 7 days. Once they have grown to approximately 2 inches (usually 2 - 3 weeks after first planting), trim at the soil line with scissors. Wash well in a fine sieve and leave to completely dry on paper towel. Can be stored in airtight bags in the fridge for around 4 days.

A

Acute Lung Tonic 94
Alkaline Potassium Soup 95
Avocado Dip with Garlic and Chilli 36

B

Baby Spinach and Capsicum Salad 57
Balsamic and Thyme Brussels Sprouts 47
Berries
 - *Margaret's Blueberry Nut Muesli 17*
 - *Sienna's Maple Berry Muesli for Kids 21*
Baked Turmeric Taro Chips 40
Beetroot
 - *Roasted Beetroot with Balsamic, Cumin and Yoghurt 45*
 - *Tangy Beetroot Salad 59*
Black Rice
 - *Glazed Salmon with Tricolor Quinoa and Black Rice 89*
Brussels Sprouts
 - *Balsamic and Thyme Brussels Sprouts 47*

C

Cabbage
 - *Red Cabbage Salad 61*
Cauliflower
 - *Cauliflower and Cumin Scramble 31*
 - *Ma Po Tofu with Eggplant and Cauliflower 83*
 - *Roasted Cauliflower, Cumin and Ginger Chicken Soup 68*
Chicken
 - *Chicken Rice Paper Rolls 24*
 - *Flavoursome Poached Chicken 28*
 - *Roasted Cauliflower, Cumin and Ginger Chicken Soup 68*
 - *Thai Chicken Curry 87*
Chick Peas
 - *Chick Pea Tuna Salad 25*
 - *Margaret's Hummus 34*

Coconut and Spinach Dahl 71
Curry
 - *Fragrant Fish Curry 81*
 - *Thai Chicken Curry 87*
 - *Vegetarian Eggplant Curry 75*

D

Dijon, Balsamic and Basil Potatoes 51
Dips
 - *Avocado Dip with Garlic and Chilli 36*
 - *Margaret's Hummus 34*
 - *Eggplant Dip 35*
 - *Dips with Celery Sticks or Rice Crackers 39*

E

Eggs
 - *Quinoa and Vegetable Scramble 18*
 - *Cauliflower and Cumin Scramble 31*
Eggplant Dip 35
Eggplant
 - *Ma Po Tofu with Eggplant and Cauliflower 83*
 - *Vegetarian Eggplant Curry 75*

F

Fennel and Radish Salad 59
Fish
 - *Fragrant Fish Curry 81*
 - *Glazed Salmon with Tricolor Quinoa and Black Rice 89*
 - *Lemon Tuna and Noodles with Vegetables and Seaweed 91*
 - *Poached Salmon with Soba Noodles and Black Sesame 74*
 - *Tuna Steak with Herb Drizzle 90*
Flavoursome Poached Chicken 28
Fragrant Fish Curry 81

G

Ginger and Garlic Gai Lan 53
Glazed Salmon with Tricolor Quinoa and
  Black Rice 89
Gluten-Free Breakfast Cereal 16
Green Papaya Salad 63

H

Home Remedies
  - *Acute Lung Tonic* 94
  - *Alkaline Potassium Soup* 95

I

Italian Style Silverbeet and Beans 42

L

Land and Sea Paella 77
Lemon Tuna and Noodles with Vegetables
  and Seaweed 91
Lentil Salad 64
Lime, Chilli and Paprika Pepitas 39
Lung
  - *Acute Lung Tonic* 94

M

Ma Po Tofu with Eggplant and Cauliflower 83
Margaret's Hummus 34
Microgreens
  - *How to grow Microgreens* 99
Muesli
  - *Margaret's Blueberry Nut Muesli* 17
  - *Sienna's Maple Berry Muesli for Kids* 21
  - *Gluten Free Breakfast Cereal* 16
  - *Yoghurt and Muesli* 19
  - *The Real Deal Muesli Bars* 38
Mushrooms
  - *Spinach and Chinese Mushrooms* 47

P

Paella
  - *Land and Sea Paella* 77
Papaya
  - *Green Papaya Salad* 63
Pepitas (Pumpkin Seeds)
  - *Lime, Chilli and Paprika Pepitas* 39
Poached Salmon with Soba Noodles and
  Black Sesame 74
Pork
  - *Rocky's Slow Cooker Pulled Pork* 79
Potatoes
  - *Dijon, Balsamic and Basil Potatoes* 51
Pumpkin seeds
  - *Lime, Chilli and Paprika Pepitas* 39

Q

Quinoa
  - *Quick Quinoa Porridge* 22
  - *Quinoa and Vegetable Scramble* 18
  - *Quinoa Sushi Rolls* 27
  - *Quinoa Tabbouleh* 60
  - *How to Cook Quinoa* 98
  - *Glazed Salmon with Tricolor Quinoa and
    Black Rice* 89

R

Radicchio
  - *Raddicchio Salad* 56
  - *Roasted Radicchio with Rocket, Balsamic and
    Goat's Cheese* 49
Radish
  - *Fennel and Radish Salad* 59
Ratatouille 43
Red Cabbage Salad 61
Rice
  - *Chicken Rice Paper Rolls* 24
  - *Turmeric and Saffron Rice* 46
  - *Glazed Salmon with Tricolor Quinoa and
    Black Rice* 89

Roasted Beetroot With Balsamic, Cumin and Yoghurt 45
Roasted Radicchio with Rocket, Balsamic and Goat's Cheese 49
Roasted Cauliflower, Cumin and Ginger Chicken Soup 68
Rocky's Slow Cooker Pulled Pork 79

S

Salad
- Baby Spinach and Capsicum Salad 57
- Chick Pea Tuna Salad 25
- Fennel and Radish Salad 59
- Green Papaya Salad 63
- Lentil Salad 64
- Quinoa Tabbouleh 60
- Radicchio Salad 56
- Red Cabbage Salad 61
- Simple Zucchini Salad 61
- Slaw 57
- Tangy Beetroot Salad 59
- Tasty Green Salad 65

Salmon
- Glazed Salmon with Tricolor Quinoa and Black Rice 89
- Poached Salmon with Soba Noodles and Black Sesame 74

San Choy Bau 85
Sienna's Maple Berry Muesli for Kids 21
Silverbeet
- Italian Style Silverbeet and Beans 42

Simple Zucchini Salad 61
Slaw 57
Soup
- Roasted Cauliflower, Cumin and Ginger Chicken Soup 68
- Coconut and Spinach Dahl 71
- Spinach and Chinese Mushrooms 47
- Watercress Soup 69

Spinach and Chinese Mushrooms 47

Spinach
- Baby Spinach and Capsicum Salad 57
- Coconut and Spinach Dahl 71
- Spinach and Chinese Mushrooms 47

T

Tabbouleh
- Quinoa Tabbouleh 60

Tamari Silken Tofu 29
Tangy Beetroot Salad 59
Tasty Green Salad 65
Thai Chicken Curry 87
The Real Deal Muesli Bars 38
Tofu
- Tamari Silken Tofu 29
- Ma Po Tofu with Eggplant and Cauliflower 83

Tuna
- Tuna Steak with Herb Drizzle 90
- Lemon Tuna and Noodles with Vegetables and Seaweed 91

Turkey
- San Choy Bau 85

Turmeric and Saffron Rice 46
Taro
- Baked Turmeric Taro Chips 40

V

Vegetarian Eggplant Curry 75

W

Watercress Soup 69

Y

Yoghurt and Muesli 19

Z

Zucchini
- Simple Zucchini Salad 61

Margaret Boyd-Squires
— NATUROPATH —

www.preventdiseasecookbook.com

@MargaretBoydSquiresNaturopath

margaretboydsquiresnaturopath

www.margaretboydsquires.com.au

www.ingramcontent.com/pod-product-compliance
Lightning Source LLC
Chambersburg PA
CBHW061757290426
44109CB00030B/2883